FASHION IT!

with Lizzie McGUiRE

MY FRIENDS ALWAYS WANT TO WEAR MY CLOTHES!

Editor: Carol Field Dahlstrom
Project Editor: Paula Marshall
Writer and Project Designer: Susan M. Banker
Designer: Angie Haupert Hoogensen
Copy Chief: Terri Fredrickson
Publishing Operations Manager: Karen Schirm
Book Production Managers: Pam Kvitne, Marjorie J. Schenkelberg,
Rick von Holdt, Mark Weaver
Contributing Copy Editors: Amanda Knief, Nancy Ruhling
Contributing Proofreaders: Callie Dunbar, Sara Henderson
Technical Illustrator: Chris Neubauer Graphics, Inc.
Project Designer: Alice Wetzel
Editorial Assistant: Cheryl Eckert
Edit and Design Production Coordinator: Mary Lee Gavin

Meredith® Books
Editor in Chief: Linda Raglan Cunningham
Design Director: Matt Strelecki
Managing Editor: Gregory H. Kayko
Executive Editor, Decorating and Home Design: Denise L. Caringer

Publisher: James D. Blume
Executive Director, Marketing: Jeffrey Myers
Executive Director, New Business Development: Todd M. Davis
Executive Director, Sales: Ken Zagor
Director, Operations: George A. Susral
Director, Production: Douglas M. Johnston
Business Director: Jim Leonard

Vice President and General Manager: Douglas J. Guendel

Meredith Publishing Group
President, Publishing Group: Stephen M. Lacy
Vice President-Publishing Director: Bob Mate

Meredith Corporation
Chairman and Chief Executive Officer: William T. Kerr

In Memoriam: E.T. Meredith III (1933–2003)

Disney Publishing Worldwide, Inc.
Lisa Gerstel

Visit Lizzie every day at DisneyChannel.com

Library of Congress Control Number: 2004107515
ISBN: 0-696-22279-5

We welcome your comments and suggestions. Write to us at:
Meredith Books, Crafts Editorial Department, 1716 Locust Street–LN120,
Des Moines, IA 50309-3023. Or visit us at: meredithbooks.com

FASHION IT!
with Lizzie
McGUIRE

CONTENTS

MIRROR, MIRROR ON THE WALL, AM I THE MOST STYLIN' ONE OF ALL?

LizziE McGUiRE

a note from Lizzie!

Hi there, fellow fashion bug!

I love to shop! OK, maybe not for groceries or bathroom tile. Let me rephrase. I LOVE to shop for ME and look cool! I live to shop for clothes, jewelry, shoes—what possibly could be more fun than that? You guessed it—MAKING your own cool fashions.

I've had a blast trying fun new ways to jazz up my wardrobe with paint, dye, beads, and other neat stuff. And I'm going to share all of my secret ideas with YOU!

You'll be the talk of the class when you show up in bright tie-dyed shirts, jeans with fabric flowers, beaded jewelry—all kinds of awesome stuff you won't find in any store.

Get ready to have "glamour do" days every day by wearing excellent clothes and accessories you make yourself!

Let's get stylin'!

MY FRIEND BORROWED MY HAND-DYED T-SHIRT AND NOW SHE SAYS SHE CAN'T FIND IT. YEAH, RIGHT!

Lizzie McGuire's "What's Your Style?" Quiz!

Being a girl is extremely awesome! There are so many sides to your personality that let you act and feel differently every day. Take this quiz and see "who you are"—for today at least!

#1 — My very favorite outfit is:

A A tie-dyed shirt and worn-out jeans.
B A miniskirt and a cropped tank top.
C An angora sweater set and matching capri pants.

Write down your points! A=1, B=2, C=3.

#2 — My favorite color is:

A Red because it makes me feel powerful!
B Magenta because it matches my hair.
C Glittery pink like all my fingernails.

Write down your points! A=3, B=1, C=2.

#3 — I love flowers because:

A I like to experiment with seeds and watch them grow.
B They remind me of my favorite perfume.
C I can string them to wear as a belt.

5

Write down your points! A=3, B=2, C=1.

#4—I like to wear lip gloss:

A With flecks of glitter in the color.

B Only on special occasions.

C In soft shades of pink.

Write down your points! A=1, B=3, C=2.

#5—My favorite style of purse is:

A Any one that has a pocket for my cell phone.

B Leather with a long strap.

C One I made from beads and twine.

Write down your points! A=2, B=3, C=1.

MY MOM IS THE BEST! SHE GOT ME TWO PAIRS OF JEANS TO PAINT!

#6—If I could buy any pair of shoes, I'd pick:

A Strappy purple shoes with 4-inch heels.

B Leather sandals made from natural materials.

C Cool, colorful tennis shoes that let me move fast.

Write down your points! A=2, B=1, C=3.

#7—I like jeans because:

A They look perfect with my hand-painted shirts.

B They're ready to wear right out of the dryer—no ironing needed.

C There's always a new "in" style at my favorite store.

fashion. all over it!

Write down your points! A=1, B=3, C=2.

#8—I think hats are awesome because:

A. I can pin my "girl power" button on them.

B. They save me from bad hair days.

C. I feel like the First Lady when I wear them.

Write down your points! A=1, B=2, C=3.

#9—My favorite style of belt is:

A. A clunky, chunky chain.

B. Whatever matches my newest shirt.

C. Pink leather with silver stars.

Write down your points! A=1, B=3, C=2.

#10—When it is cold outside, I like to wear:

ACTUALLY, WHEN IT'S COLD OUTSIDE, I'D LIKE TO HEAD TO HAWAII...

A. A leather jacket and groovy knit hat.

B. A cool coat I got at a used-clothing shop.

C. Jeans and my school sweatshirt.

Write down your points! A=3, B=1, C=2.

#11—When it is hot outside, I like to wear:

A. An off-the-shoulder top with a miniskirt.

B. A T-shirt and shorts.

C. My bikini and rings on all of my toes.

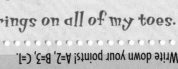

Write down your points! A=2, B=3, C=1.

#12—I like to wear sunglasses because:

A They hide the dark circles under my eyes from my best friend's sleepover.

B They look cool on me and protect my eyes from the sun.

C I look so totally '70s.

Write down your points! A=2, B=3, C=1.

Now total your quiz points.

If they total 29-36, you are
Head of the Class!

Maybe you prefer reading rather than rollerblading, and writing for the school paper over basketball. That's OK! Girls look up to you as a leader, and you're just the type to take charge!

If your points total 20-28, you are a
Social Butterfly!

You probably love dances, parties, and lunch—because the more people around, the better! With your outgoing personality, you'll never have to worry about having friends. (You'll have more of a problem remembering all their names!)

If your points total 12-19, you are a
Free Spirit!

If you enjoy your individuality and express it openly, then you are a free spirit! You will follow your dreams and live happily ever after!

Keep in mind that each time you take the quiz, you may get a different score. That's OK, 'cause that's just one of the cool things about being a girl! Now, find a project that matches your personality of the day and have fun making your own fashion statement!

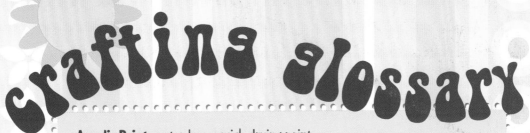

Acrylic Paint–water-base, quick-drying paint that cleans up with soap and water.

Disposable–something meant to be used once, then thrown away.

Fringe–a border or trimming of fabric, cords, or threads, hanging loose or tied in bunches.

Gems–while there are real gemstones and pearls, projects in crafting usually use plastic gems in all colors that are backed with a silver color to make them sparkle.

Horizontally–left to right, like the horizon.

Pony Beads–colorful plastic beads (round and other shapes) with a large hole in the center, ranging in size from a pea to a nickel.

Rhinestone–a colorless, bright, artificial gem made of hard glass that is often cut to look like a diamond.

Seed Beads–beads about the size of a pinhead that come in dozens of colors.

Textile Medium–a milky liquid that mixes with acrylic paint to make the paint bond with fabric.

Texture–the appearance or feel of a surface.

Tracing Paper–a thin sheet of paper that can be seen through when put on a flat surface, such as a pattern or book.

Vertically–up and down, like buttons on a shirt.

Waxed Paper–available in rolls, this paper has a moistureproof coating on it.

MY BROTHER THOUGHT PONY BEADS WERE FANCY TRIMS FOR HORSES.

just my jeans

checkered shorts

WHAT YOU NEED

Fabric scraps; iron (optional); scissors; ruler
Fabric glue; paintbrush for glue (optional)
Denim shorts; fabric glitter paint in tube
Glitter; newspapers

HERE'S HOW

1 Cut the fabric scraps into 1½-inch squares. Ask an adult to help you use an iron to press the assorted fabric squares flat, if needed.

2 Use a paintbrush or your finger to spread a generous amount of fabric glue evenly on the back of fabric squares.

3 Place the squares around the edge of each leg until the edges are covered. Place extra squares on the belt loops or on pockets.

4 Outline the squares with fabric glitter paint. For extra sparkle, sprinkle the paint with glitter while paint is wet. Let the paint dry. Shake off excess glitter onto newspapers and pour back into the glitter container.

continued on page 12

fashion all over it!

Cut out shapes from favorite clothes you've outgrown. (Be sure to ask a parent if it's OK first!) Keep the shapes simple, such as handprints, circles, and butterflies—then glue them on comfy denims!

Hangin' Out

11

posy pants

WHAT YOU NEED

Clean, dry, pressed jeans

Tracing paper; pencil; scissors

Small and large jar lids for circle patterns

Fabric scraps; iron

Fabric glue; paintbrush

Tube glitter paint in
    green, pink, and
    metallic gold

Sequins on a string

I WONDER IF I SHOULD PAINT MY SHOES TO MATCH MY COOL JEANS?

HERE'S HOW

1. Lay your jeans on a flat work surface. Trace the jar lids and patterns, opposite, onto tracing paper and cut out. Place the patterns on fabric, trace, and cut out the shapes. The fabric circles are for the flower centers as shown in the photo on page 10.

2. Arrange the fabric shapes on the jeans. Spread an even amount of fabric glue on the back side of fabric pieces as shown in Photo A, below. Press shapes onto jeans, smoothing out any wrinkles as shown in Photo B.

3. Outline the fabric shapes using the glitter paints as shown in Photo C. Let dry.

4. For each flower stem, draw a line of fabric glue onto jeans and apply the sequins on a string, trimming off the excess. Let dry.

A

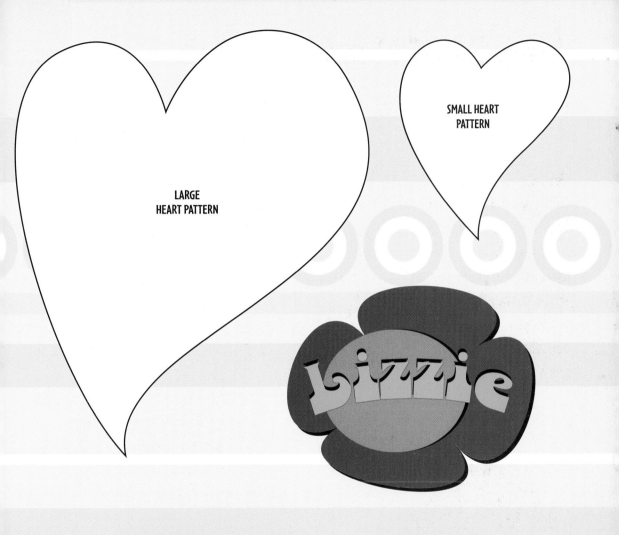

LARGE
HEART PATTERN

SMALL HEART
PATTERN

lizzie

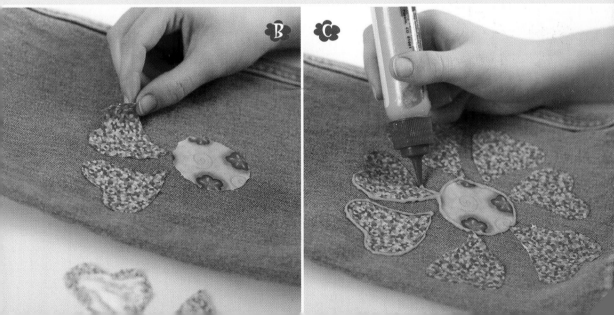

B   C

so stylin' & summery

posy platforms (left)

WHAT YOU NEED

Scissors; silk flowers
White fabric glue; seed beads
White platform thongs
Acrylic paints in purple and
   orange, or other
   desired colors
Paintbrush
Purple glitter paint

continued on page 16

SCHOOL'S COOL

fashion. all over it!

Be good to the environment!
Recycle things you otherwise
would throw away—old hair bows, earrings,
refrigerator magnets, plastic toys—by gluing
them onto your shoes!

Seriously Cool!

HERE'S HOW

1. Trim plastic stem off of flower. If the flower comes apart, glue the layers of silk petals back together as shown in Photo A, opposite. Let dry.

2. Place a generous amount of glue in center of flower, and pour just enough seed beads onto glue to cover as shown in Photo B. Let dry.

3. Paint the platform sides of thongs with orange paint. Let dry.

4. Use purple paint to create stripes, circles, or other simple designs on the shoe platforms. Let dry.

5. Paint glitter paint over the purple painted areas for extra sparkle. Let dry.

6. Use a generous amount of white glue to attach flower to the thong.

sequined sandals (page 15)

WHAT YOU NEED

Slide sandals

Fabric glue

Glitter

2 purchased sequined flower appliqués

HERE'S HOW

1. Spread a generous amount of glue on the back side of the sequin appliqués and apply to sandals. Let the glue dry.

2. Outline the edge trim of the sandal soles with a generous amount of glue. Sprinkle glitter on the glue until well covered as shown in Photo C. Let dry. Shake off the extra glitter.

NOW THAT I KNOW HOW TO IRON, MOM HAS ADDED IT TO MY LIST OF CHORES.

SCHOOL'S COOL

Get a designer look in minutes ironing colorful flowers on a shirt.

irresistible iron-ons

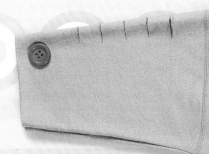

orange original (left)

WHAT YOU NEED

Floral iron-ons from the back pages of this book

Small round lid; scissors

Light orange scoop-neck shirt (50% cotton/50% polyester works best)

Iron; small buttons in blue and green; fabric glue

continued on page 20

HANGIN' OUT

fashion. all over it!

Your friends won't believe you made these supercool shirts! Show them how easy it is (with Mom's help) and have a girls-only, get-creative, shirt-making party!

19

HERE'S HOW

1 Tear out the desired iron-on sheet from the back pages of this book. Leaving a small border around each design, cut out the flowers. To cut circles around the shapes, trace around small jar lid or other round object before cutting.

2 Using the photo on page 18 as a guide, place the iron-ons

right-side down on the shirt. Ask an adult to help you slowly iron on the back side of the designs on high for no more than 1 minute, keeping the iron moving. Let cool. Lift off the backing paper.

3 Embellish the shirt by gluing buttons on and between the collar iron-ons, and in the center of the large flower as shown on page 18. Glue buttons in the shape of a leaf by the large flower. Let the glue dry.

❁ ❁ ❁

purple pizzazz

WHAT YOU NEED

Lavender sweatshirt (50% cotton/50% polyester works best); scissors

Floral iron-ons from the back pages of this book

Small and large jar lids; iron

Assorted buttons in various colors; fabric glue

HERE'S HOW

1 Carefully cut off the banding from the hem, cuffs, and neckline of the sweatshirt.

2 Tear out the desired iron-on sheet from the back pages of this book. Cut out the flowers, leaving a small border around each design. To cut circles around the shapes, trace around a circular object before cutting.

KEEP THE IRON MOVING SO YOU DON'T SCORCH YOUR SHIRT!

20

A **B**

3 Using the photo on page 19 as a guide, place the iron-ons right-side down on the shirt. Ask an adult to help you slowly iron on the back side of the designs on high for no more than 1 minute, keeping the iron moving. Let them cool, and lift off the backing paper.

4 Decorate the shirt by gluing buttons on and around the iron-ons as shown in the photo. Let the glue dry.

5 Lay the shirt flat with the sleeve seams at the bottom. Use scissors to cut five 1-inch slits evenly spaced along the top edge of each sleeve using the photos above and on page 19 as guides.

sew-cool belts

flower parade

WHAT YOU NEED

Black canvas belt with clasp-style buckle
Thin wood assorted-color flower cutouts
  (available in craft stores)
Pinhole paper punch, such as Fiskars
Black embroidery floss; sewing needle
Black beads; scissors

HERE'S HOW

1 Lay the belt on a flat work surface. Decide how to arrange the wood flowers on the belt. Layer three flowers in varying sizes to form a decorative buckle.

continued on page 24

SCHOOL'S COOL

fashion. all over it!

Check out all the cool wood shapes at the crafts store! When you buy them to make belts, be sure the wood is thin enough to punch with a pinhole punch.

23

2 For each of the wood flowers, punch a hole in the center of the flower as shown in Photo A, opposite.

3 Thread the needle with embroidery floss. Knot one end.

4 From the back of the belt, push the needle through the belt where a flower is desired. Pull the embroidery floss so the knot is snugged up to the back of the belt. Thread on a wood flower and a bead. Push the needle back through the wood flower and into the belt as shown in Photo B. Knot the floss. Sew on the rest of the flowers and beads in the same way. Knot the embroidery floss on the back of the belt, and cut off the excess.

5 For the layered flower, push through the threaded needle from the back of the belt close to the buckle. Thread on flowers, largest to smallest. Thread on a bead and push the needle back through the wood shapes. Knot floss on belt back.

circles and squares

WHAT YOU NEED

Natural canvas belt with buckle
Thin wood squares and circles in blue and green
  (available in crafts stores)
Pinhole paper punch, such as Fiskars
Tan embroidery floss; sewing needle; scissors

HERE'S HOW

1 Lay the belt on a flat work surface. Decide how to arrange the wood shapes on the belt. Leave the end of the belt that goes through the buckle free of wood pieces.

I WONDER IF WOOD FLOWERS COME FROM WOOD SEEDS? NAH.

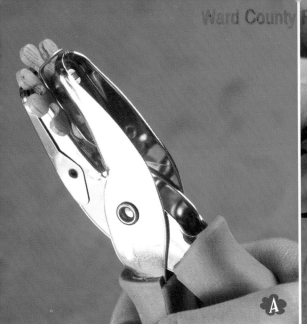

A   B

Lizzie

2 For each of the wood pieces, punch one hole in the center or two holes on opposite sides as shown in the photo on page 23.

3 Thread the needle with embroidery floss. Knot one end.

4 From the back of the belt, push the needle through the belt where a wood shape is desired. Pull the embroidery floss so the knot is snugged up to the belt. Thread on a wood piece. For a one-hole wood piece, push the needle back through the belt at one edge of the wood piece. Bring the needle up through the center of the wood piece and back down into the belt at the opposite side of the wood piece. For a two-hole wood piece, push the needle up through one hole and down through the opposite hole. Knot floss on back. Sew on the rest of the wood shapes in the same way. Knot the embroidery floss on the back of the belt. Cut off the excess.

autograph shirts

pretty in pink

WHAT YOU NEED

Disposable plates
Assorted colors of acrylic paint
Textile medium; pink cotton shirt; waxed paper
Small round and flat paintbrushes

HERE'S HOW

1 Place a small amount of each paint color on a disposable plate. As shown in Photo A on page 29, use a paintbrush to mix each color with textile medium, following the label directions.

continued on page 28

HANGIN' OUT

fashion. all over it!

It's easy to paint words on a shirt with a paintbrush and acrylic paint! You also may paint a short poem, a favorite quote, or the name of your school on your shirt.

2 Lay the shirt on a flat work surface. Place a piece of waxed paper inside the shirt. Ask your friends to paint their names horizontally on the front of the shirt, allowing them to make the names different sizes and colors. See Photo B, opposite. To avoid smears, ask your friends to start at the top of the shirt and work downward. Let the paint dry.

3 For large names, add extra color to the letters with painted dots and dotted lines. Let dry.

4 Fill in the blank areas with painted shapes, such as hearts and stars. Let the paint dry.

not-so-mellow yellow graffiti top

WHAT YOU NEED

Disposable plate
Black acrylic paint; textile medium
Yellow lace-up cotton shirt
Waxed paper
Small round and flat paintbrushes
Black fabric marking pen

HERE'S HOW

1 Place a small amount of black paint on a disposable plate. As shown using colored paint in Photo A, opposite, use a paintbrush to mix the paint with textile medium, following the label directions.

2 Lay your shirt on a flat work surface. Place a piece of waxed paper inside the shirt. Ask your friends to paint their names horizontally or vertically on the front of the shirt, allowing them to make the names different sizes. See Photo B,

I'M GOING TO MAKE SHIRTS FOR MY WHOLE FAMILY— EVEN MY BROTHER!

above. To avoid smears, ask your friends to start at the top of the shirt and work downward. Let dry.

3 To write names smaller than those done with a paintbrush, let your friends use a fabric marking pen. Use the pen to add shapes such as flower petals, swirls, and hearts to the open areas and around the lace holes.

to-dye-for duds

color-splashed pants, tank, and shirt set (left)

WHAT YOU NEED

Iron; white cotton pants and shirt

Coordinating tank top

Waxed paper

Crafts foam stickers in
  flower and heart shapes

Small plastic spray bottles

Fabric dyes, such as Dye-na-Flow,
  in purple, green, blue, and pink
  (available in the fabric paint section of crafts
  stores), or other colors you like

Water; white paper; glitter paint in tube

Paintbrush; fabric paints in colors to coordinate
  with dye colors; fine glitter (optional)

Hair dryer

HANGIN' OUT

continued on page 32

fashion. all over it!

You could start your own business making bright-painted clothes or at least make supercool birthday presents for your friends! Watch for sales on plain clothing, and put your creativity to work!

31

Arrange the pants and shirt in a single layer on the work surface, keeping as flat and smooth as possible because wrinkles and folds will show up after painting. Insert a piece of white paper between clothing layers to prevent the paint from soaking through.

Experiment overlapping the dye colors on white paper before spraying clothing. (If you chose other dye colors, use the Color Wheel on page 35 as a guide for blending.) When you like the way it looks, spray quick bursts of color on the shirt as shown in Photos B and C, overlapping slightly to blend one color to the next. It's important to spray quick bursts of paint holding the bottle 8 to 10 inches from the fabric. Avoid totally soaking the fabric or it will bleed too much under your sticker patterns. To darken colors, let the dye dry and apply a second coat. Use a hair dryer to speed the drying time. Let dry. Remove the stickers as shown in Photo D.

HERE'S HOW

1 Ask an adult to wash, dry, and iron the clothing. Cover a flat work surface with waxed paper. Lay the clothing on the protected work surface.

2 Peel off the paper backing from foam stickers, as shown in Photo A, opposite, and place randomly on the lower parts of the shirt and pants.

3 For each dye color, mix about 1 tablespoon of dye with 2 tablespoons of water in a spray bottle.

I'LL MAKE A MATCHING BEACH TOTE AND COVER-UP AND BE THE ENVY OF THE POOL!

6 To decorate the tank top, opposite, use a foam sticker and brush a generous amount of fabric paint onto the non-sticky foam side. Press it onto the fabric and remove. Let dry. Brush on additional paint if you wish. Let dry.

7 Outline the shapes with glitter paint. For larger areas spread glitter paint with a brush. If desired, for more shine, sprinkle very fine glitter into the wet glitter paint. Let dry.

forever hearts and flowers
shorts set (page 31)

WHAT YOU NEED

Iron; white or light-color cotton shirt and shorts
Waxed paper
Crafts foam stickers in various shapes, including
  hearts and flowers
Small plastic spray bottles; hair dryer
Fabric dyes, such as Dye-na-Flow, in red and yellow
  or other colors you like; water; white paper
Glitter paint in tube to coordinate with dye colors
Paintbrush; fabric paints to coordinate with dye
  colors for shorts; fine glitter (optional)

HERE'S HOW

1 Ask an adult to wash, dry, and iron the
  clothing. Cover a flat work surface with
waxed paper. Lay the clothing on the protected
work surface.

2 Peel off the paper backing from foam
  stickers, as shown in Photo A on page 33,
and place randomly on the shirt leaving space
between the stickers.

3 For each dye color, mix about
  1 tablespoon of dye with 2 tablespoons
of water in a spray bottle.

4 Lay the shirt in a single layer on the work
  surface, keeping as flat and smooth as
possible because wrinkles and folds will show up
after painting. Slip white paper between the shirt
layers to prevent paint from soaking through.

5 Experiment overlapping the dye colors on
  paper before spraying clothing. (If you
choose other dye colors, use the Color Wheel,
opposite, as a guide for blending.) When you like
the way it looks, spray quick bursts of color on the
shirt as shown in Photos B and C on page 33,
overlapping slightly to blend one color to the next.
It is important to spray quick bursts of paint
holding the bottle 8 to 10 inches from the fabric.
Avoid totally soaking the fabric or it will bleed too
much under your stickers. To darken colors, let the
dye dry and apply a second coat. Use a hair dryer
to speed the drying time. Let dry. Remove the
stickers as shown in Photo D on page 33.

6 To paint the shorts, use a foam sticker
  and brush a generous amount of paint
onto the non-sticky foam side. Press it onto the
fabric and remove. Let dry. Brush on additional
paint if you wish. Let dry.

7 Outline the shapes with glitter paint. For
  larger areas, spread on the glitter paint
with a paintbrush. If desired, for more shine,
sprinkle very fine glitter into the wet glitter paint.
Let dry.

color wheel

The color wheel shows why some colors work together while others seem to clash. Colors that sit next to one another on the wheel blend nicely.

Primary Colors: Yellow, red, and blue

Secondary Colors: Orange, violet, green (halfway between primary colors on the color wheel)

Tertiary Colors: Yellow-orange, red-orange, red-violet, blue-violet, blue-green, yellow-green (between primary and secondary colors on the color wheel)

Neutral Tones: White, gray, black, and beige

Tint: Made by adding white to a color (for example, pink is a tint of red)

Shade: Made by adding black to a color (for example, maroon is a shade of red)

Yellow + red = orange

Red + blue = purple

Blue + yellow = green

Yellow + orange = yellow-orange

Orange + red = red-orange

Red + purple = red-violet

Purple + blue = blue-violet

Blue + green = blue-green

Green + yellow = yellow-green

35

SCHOOL'S COOL

WHAT YOU NEED

Tracing paper; pencil; scissors
Velour fabric in blue or pink
Imitation suede; fabric glue
Beaded trim to coordinate with fabric
Flower appliqué and/or sequins
Beading needle
Beading elastic
Seed beads to match fabric

BARE FEET HAVE NEVER LOOKED SO GOOD!

Fabric foot trims look super-cool when you glue on sparkling accents.

foot thongs

HERE'S HOW

1 Trace the triangle pattern, below, onto tracing paper; cut out. Trace around the pattern on the fabric and suede; cut out. Wrong sides facing, glue the triangles together.

2 Cut the bead trim to fit the long edges of the triangle. Spread glue on the back of the trim. Place under the fabric edge; press firmly.

3 For the blue thong, left, glue the appliqué in the center of the thong. Glue sequins on the appliqué. For the pink thong, right, glue sequins on the fabric. Let dry.

4 For the toe loop, thread elastic into the needle. Stitch the elastic to the long tip of the fabric triangle, knotting to secure. Thread 1½ inches with beads. Check fit by wrapping beaded elastic around your second toe. Add or subtract beads if necessary. Stitch elastic through tip of triangle; knot and cut off excess.

5 For ankle loop, repeat Step 4, using enough elastic and beads to fit around your ankle from the opposite tips of the triangle.

HANGIN' OUT

TRIANGLE PATTERN

Old or new, floral or graphic, bright or soft, handkerchiefs and bandannas add a girly touch to shirts.

SCHOOL'S COOL

I CAN IRON AND SEW! I THINK I'M READY FOR MY OWN APARTMENT!

hot tops

buttons and bows hankie top

WHAT YOU NEED

Cotton $^3/_4$-length sleeve V-neck shirt; iron
3 or more assorted cotton hankies, new or vintage
Ruler; pencil; needle; thread; iron-on hem tape
Scissors; five $^1/_2$-inch buttons; two 1-inch buttons
Two $^3/_4$-inch buttons; $^1/_8$-inch ribbon in two colors

HANGIN' OUT

HERE'S HOW

1. **Note:** You will need to use an iron a lot for this project; be sure to ask an adult for help. If needed, iron the shirt and hankies.

2. To cut the hankies into triangles for the collar and sleeves, use a ruler and pencil to make a mark up two sides of one hanky, 7 inches from one corner. Use a ruler to draw a line between the markings. Cut along the line. Repeat marking and cutting steps for all hankies to get two matching triangles for the collar and three for each sleeve.

3. For the sleeve hankies, with the wrong sides together, fold over $^1/_4$ inch along the cut edge and iron to crease. Thread the needle. Knot the

continued on page 40

fashion all over it!

Ironing is easy! Just be sure to follow these smarty pants rules: Always ask an adult to help. Never leave an iron unattended. Be careful, it gets HOT! Be sure to turn it off AND unplug it when you're done.

39

thread end. Stitch gathering stitches $1/8$ inch from the fold as shown in Photo A, opposite. Pull the thread to slightly gather the hanky; knot thread and cut off the extra. Repeat with the remaining five sleeve hankies.

4 Turn shirt inside out. Cut hem tape to fit around each cuff area. Place the gathered edge of one scarf piece on tape; iron to stick it to the shirt as shown in Photo B. Repeat, overlapping two more hanky pieces. Repeat for other sleeve.

5 For the two collar hankies, with wrong sides together, fold over 1 inch along the cut edge and iron to crease. Following the manufacturer's directions for the hem tape, attach the folded over areas to each side of the V-neck as shown in Photo C. This is called fusing. Turn shirt right-side out.

6 Referring to page 79, sew three $1/2$-inch buttons down the shirt front. Layer and sew 1- and $3/4$-inch buttons on each collar. Sew a $1/2$-inch button to each cuff. Cut two 18-inch lengths of each ribbon. Tie two ribbons around cuff buttons.

bandanna tank top (page 39)

WHAT YOU NEED

Cotton tank top; iron; bandannas in two colors Ruler; pencil; scissors; straight pins; iron-on hem tape Three black 1-inch buttons; 1-inch-wide braid to coordinate with bandannas; needle; thread Three $1/2$-inch color buttons

HERE'S HOW

1 **Note:** You will need to use an iron a lot for this project; be sure to ask an adult for help. If needed, iron the tank top and bandannas.

2 To cut the bandanna triangles, use a ruler and pencil to make marks up each side of one bandanna, 9 inches from one corner. Use the ruler to draw a line between the markings. Cut along the line. Repeat this step, cutting two triangles from the other bandanna color.

3 Overlap bandannas in a vertical row, using the photo on page 39 as a guide; pin together. Cut pieces of iron-on hem tape to fit the length of the bandannas and the sides of each bandanna triangle. Position the tape on the wrong side of the bandannas as shown in Photo D, opposite.

4 Tape side down, place the bandannas on the tank top. Following the manufacturer's directions for the hem tape, iron the bandannas to stick them to the tank top as shown in Photo E. This is called fusing. Remove the pins.

5 Cut a piece of braid 2 inches longer than the length of tank top. Place hem tape along cut edges of the bandannas. Place braid centered on the tape, and iron in place as shown in Photo F. Fold the ends of the braid to the back side of the shirt on top and under at the bottom; fuse in place using small pieces of hem tape.

6 Layer a small and large button. Referring to page 79, sew buttons to each bandanna tip.

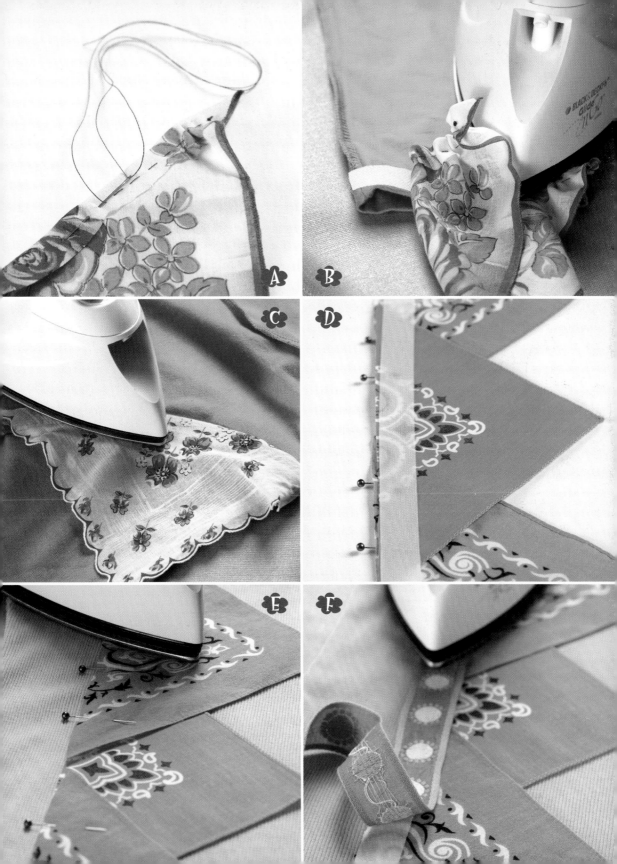

happenin' hats

flashy and fancy (left)

WHAT YOU NEED

Black beret-style hat with brim

Pink puff fabric paint in tube

Paintbrush; fine pink glitter

Hair dryer

3 yards of pink
  ribbon

Scissors

Safety pin or needle
  and thread

continued on page 44

fashion. all over it!

There are a zillion kinds of hats! There is the type with a wide brim to keep out the sun. There are fancy hats for superdressy occasions. There are hats with tassels, bills, fringes, pom-poms, and bands. There are hats made of straw, fabric, leather, and yarn. What kind of hat girl are you today?

inches from the paint until it begins to puff up. If your hair dryer gets extremely hot, move it back and forth so you don't burn yourself or the hat.

4 Cut off 1 yard of ribbon. Fold it back and forth (accordion-style) about 6 inches. Cut a 6-inch piece of ribbon and tie the bundle of ribbon in the middle. Cut the ends of the loops.

5 Fold the end of the ribbon in half and cut an angle from the fold upward to the outer edge to make a V shape.

I'M GOING TO WEAR MY NEW HAT ON MY FIELD TRIP—HOW AWESOME IS THAT?!

HERE'S HOW

1 Use puff paint to draw circles, lines, or any design you wish on the hat top as shown in Photo A, opposite. Use a paintbrush to generously cover the bill of the hat with puff paint.

2 Sprinkle fine glitter onto the wet paint and let it dry. This may take several hours.

3 Use a hair dryer set on high to puff the paint as shown in Photo B. Hold it several

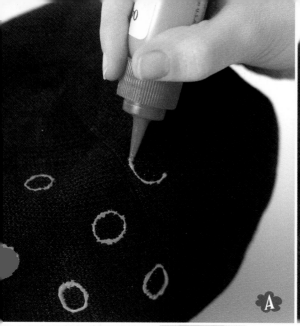

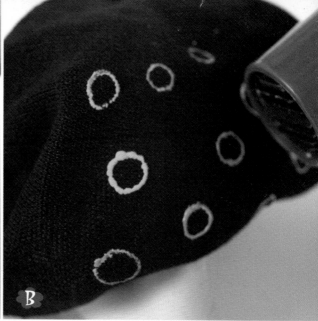

6 To make the long tails, tie the remaining pieces of ribbon around the center of the bow. Trim the ends into V shapes.

7 Use a safety pin or needle and thread to attach the bow to the back of the hat.

❀❀❀❀

at-the-beach casual (page 43)

WHAT YOU NEED

Fabric hat; puff tube paints in colors you like
Hair dryer; large crafts foam floral sticker
Large button; crafts glue

HERE'S HOW

1 Use puff paints to draw simple borders, such as dots and wavy lines, around the hat as shown in the photo on page 43. Let the paint dry.

2 Use a hair dryer set on high to puff the paint. Hold it several inches from the paint until it begins to puff up. If your hair dryer gets extremely hot, move it back and forth so you don't burn yourself or the hat.

3 Peel the backing off the floral sticker and press sticker onto hat. Glue a button in the center of the flower. Fill in the button holes with puff paint. Let the paint dry.

Seriously cool!

color-burst shirts

pretty pastel tank top (left)

WHAT YOU NEED

White tank top; tie-dye kit
Bucket; tube-style fabric paint

HERE'S HOW

1 To tie-dye the shirt, follow the directions in the tie-dye kit. To make the pattern on the shirt, opposite,

continued on page 48

SCHOOL'S COOL

fashion. all over it!
Tie-dying is so much fun because no two projects turn out alike, and each one is a surprise when you take off the rubber bands! Just be sure to wear old clothes when you're using dye.

47

twist the shirt fabric, as shown in Photo A, opposite, in several places. Wrap rubber bands around each bundle.

2 Dye the wrapped shirt using very little dye and following the manufacturer's directions. Rinse, wash, and dry the shirt.

3 Use tube paint to draw a scallop and dots around the neckline, as shown on page 46.

beaded-hem T-shirt (page 47)

WHAT YOU NEED

White T-shirt with red banding trim
Tie-dye kit; bucket
Scissors; red pony beads

HERE'S HOW

1 To tie-dye the shirt, follow the directions in the tie-dye kit. To make the pattern on the shirt shown on page 47, make horizontal folds in the shirt starting at the hem as shown in Photo B, opposite. Wrap rubber bands around the bundle.

2 Squirt red and blue dye on the shirt following the manufacturer's directions. (See Photo C.) Rinse, wash, and dry the shirt.

3 Cut off the bottom hem. Making fringes 1 inch apart, cut a 3-inch-long fringe all around the bottom of the shirt.

4 Slide a pony bead up each fringe. Tie a knot below each bead to hold it in place.

seriously cool

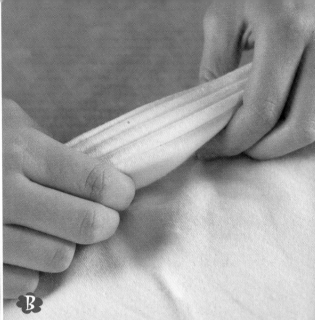

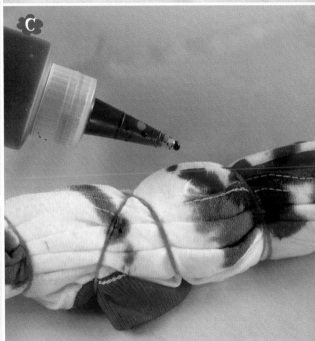

A

B

C

I'D LOVE TO HAVE A TIE-DYING PARTY WITH ALL OF MY FRIENDS...

darn-cute denims

very cool vest

WHAT YOU NEED

Denim vest; iron and ironing board (optional)

Glitter fabric paint in a color you like

Small flat paintbrush; disposable plate

Glitter paint in tube; gems

Seed beads

Newspapers

continued on page 56

fashion. all over it! Denim clothes are so neat to paint. To coat them in color, look at the seam lines and use them as guides for your designs. You can follow the shapes or simply use them to divide blocks of color.

HANGIN' OUT

HERE'S HOW

1 Begin with a clean, dry, and pressed vest. Lay the vest on a flat, newspaper-covered surface.

2 Pour a small amount of fabric paint onto a disposable plate. Using the seams as guides, use fabric paint to outline a section on the vest. Paint stripes within the outlines as shown in Photo A, opposite. Let the paint dry. Apply a second coat if needed.

3 To add gems, apply a generous amount of glitter tube paint to vest and buttons; press gems into wet paint as shown in Photo B. Sprinkle seed beads in wet paint. Add dots of glue to the vest; sprinkle with beads. Let dry.

color-block jacket (page 55)

WHAT YOU NEED

Denim jacket
Iron and ironing board (optional)
Fabric paints in colors you like
Fabric painting brush
Circular objects; pencil
Glitter paint in tube; gems

HERE'S HOW

1 Begin with a clean, dry, and pressed jacket. Lay jacket on a flat, newspaper-covered surface.

2 Use a fabric painting brush to paint sections of the jacket. When painting light colors, paint the area with white, let dry, and then apply color. Let dry. Apply a second coat to areas where heavier coverage or a darker color is desired.

3 Paint contrasting circles, stripes, or other shapes on the solid painted areas. To

MY JEAN JACKET NEVER SEES MY LOCKER—I WEAR IT ALL DAY LONG!

56

A   B

make circles, trace round objects with a pencil and fill in with paint. Let dry.

4   To add gems, apply a generous amount of glitter paint to jacket and press gems into wet paint. Let dry.

Lizzie

Embroidery floss comes in every color under the sun—so pick your favorites to make the prettiest bracelets on earth!

SCHOOL'S COOL

BE SURE TO ASK BEFORE SNEAKING FLOSS FROM YOUR MOM'S SEWING BASKET!

bracelet trio

WHAT YOU NEED

Scissors
Bright colors of embroidery floss
3 thin plastic bangle bracelets
Thick white crafts glue

HERE'S HOW

1 For a solid-color bracelet, cut a 36-inch length of embroidery floss.

2 Working on small sections at a time, put a thin layer of glue on the bracelet.

floss-wrapped bracelets

3 Wrap floss tightly around the area with glue on the bracelet. Glue floss around the bracelet until it is covered, using more floss if needed.

4 For the multicolor bangle, wrap and glue the small areas of color first. Fill in between the wrapped areas with another color of floss. Let the glue dry.

❋✿❋

bright bangle

WHAT YOU NEED

Scissors; variegated (different shades of one color in one strand) embroidery floss in red, blue, green, and yellow; black embroidery floss
Thick plastic bangle bracelet
Thick white crafts glue

HERE'S HOW

1 Cut two 14-inch lengths from each variegated color of embroidery floss.

2 Working on small sections at a time, put a thin layer of glue on the bracelet.

3 Begin with one color of variegated floss and wrap tightly around the glued area on the bracelet. Continue gluing floss around the bracelet, alternating colors, until the bracelet is covered, cutting more 14-inch pieces if needed.

4 Cut a 20-inch length of black floss. Glue one end of the floss to the inside of the floss-covered bracelet. Wrap and glue the floss around the bracelet, letting the colors show through. Trim off the extra floss and glue the end to the bracelet. Let the glue dry.

HANGIN' OUT

59

girly green

WHAT YOU NEED

Beading string; 2 heart beads

Silver beads; silver floral spacer beads

Two shades of green seed beads

Beading needle; ruler

Decorative center bead with 4 holes

Bead a long style of necklace that has nifty long tails and pretty connectors.

> I AM SO HOOKED ON BEADING MY FRIENDS CALL ME BEADING BEAUTY!

HERE'S HOW

1 Tie a seed bead onto one end of the beading string. Tie several tight knots.

2 Thread the string onto a beading needle, pulling through about 8 inches of thread.

3 The first 5 inches you string will become the first tail of the necklace. Begin with a heart bead, a silver bead, and then alternate the two colors of seed beads.

4 Insert the needle and thread through the bottom of the decorative center bead and out through the top.

5 Continue stringing beads in whatever pattern you wish until you have strung another 23 inches.

Cutie-pie Ys

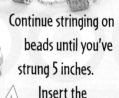

This size should fit over your head without needing a clasp. Check it for fit before moving on to the next step.

6 When you have enough length in your necklace, push the thread through the top of the center bead.

7 Finish stringing the remaining tail like the other one and tie the last bead on with a very tight knot. Push the end of string back up through several beads to make it extra secure. Trim off extra thread.

soft hues

WHAT YOU NEED

Beading string; seed beads
Beading needle; ruler; bell caps
Assorted beads; spacer beads; triangle bead

HERE'S HOW

1 Tie a seed bead onto one end of the beading string. Tie several tight knots.

2 Thread the string onto a beading needle, pulling through about 8 inches of thread.

3 The first 5 inches you string will become the bottom of the tail of necklace. Begin with a bell cap, a large bead, and another bell cap.

Continue stringing on beads until you've strung 5 inches.

4 Insert the needle and thread through the bottom of the triangle center bead and out through the top.

5 Continue stringing beads in whatever pattern you wish until you have strung another 23 inches. This size should fit over your head without needing a clasp. Check it for fit before continuing to the next step.

6 When your necklace is long enough, insert the thread back through the top of the bead and down through the bottom.

7 String the remaining tail like the first one. Tie the last bead on with a tight knot. Push the end of the string back up through several beads to make it secure. Trim off the extra thread.

COOL! MOM WANTS A WRAP BRACELET IN ALL OF OUR BIRTHSTONE COLORS.

Make a fancy bracelet on a wire that always remembers how to wrap around your wrist.

black coil bracelet

WHAT YOU NEED

Memory wire for bracelet (precoiled, available in crafts stores); wire cutters

Round-nose pliers; end beads

Silver spacer beads; charm

Large black seed beads; colored accent beads

HERE'S HOW

1 Use wire cutters to trim the memory wire to the length you wish.

2 Use round-nose pliers to make a loop at one end of the wire. Make the loop large enough to hold the end bead in place. Trim off extra wire.

wonderful wrist wraps

3 Place the end bead on, then a spacer, the charm, and another spacer.

4 Begin placing remaining beads on in whatever pattern you wish.

5 When you have about $1/2$ inch remaining, place the end bead on, and use the pliers to make a tight loop to hold the beads in place. Use the wire cutters to trim off extra wire.

❋ ❋ ❋ ❋

red coil bracelet

WHAT YOU NEED

Memory wire for bracelet (precoiled, available in crafts stores); wire cutters; round-nose pliers
End beads; large assorted seed beads; small charms

HERE'S HOW

1 Use wire cutters to trim the memory wire to the length you wish.

2 Use round-nose pliers to make a loop at one end of the wire. Make the loop large enough to hold the end bead in place. Trim off the extra wire.

3 Place the first end bead on, then the large seed beads. Add a charm and more seed beads. Continue adding beads in the same pattern.

4 When you have about $1/2$ inch remaining, place the end bead on, and use the pliers to make a tight loop to hold the beads in place. Use the wire cutters to trim off extra wire.

Whether you like to wear hip ties or scarves, this paint and foil project will have you tied in style!

SCHOOL'S COOL

I'M GOING TO PUT MY SCARF THROUGH MY JEAN LOOPS AND WEAR IT AS A BELT!

nifty neckties

funky flower scarf (left)

WHAT YOU NEED

Patterned scarf (available at clothing stores); tape
Foil adhesive; crafting foil (available in crafts stores)
White glitter fabric dimensional tube paint
Hot pink glitter

HERE'S HOW

1 Lay scarf on flat work surface, and tape the scarf edges to the work surface. If your scarf is thin, the adhesive will bleed through, so do not put the scarf on paper or cardboard because the scarf will stick to it.

continued on page 66

fashion. all over it!

Get ready to make a fashion statement by wearing a scarf or tie made by you! These projects show two neat designs but use your imagination to decorate your wardrobe accessory any way you like!

2 Use the adhesive in a squirt bottle to draw flower designs to be foiled as shown in Photo A, opposite. You can draw dots, lines, simple shapes, or your initials. The adhesive will look milky white. When it is dry and ready for foiling it will appear clear and feel tacky. Be careful as you draw. You cannot wipe it off easily and the foil will stick wherever you put adhesive. Do not move to the next step before it dries; it is important to do these in order.

3 Lay dull side of foil onto tacky dry adhesive; rub it gently but firmly until all foil sticks to adhesive. Pull away the sheet, leaving the design foil-embossed as shown in Photo B.

4 Draw in flower petals using white glitter paint as shown in Photo C. Sprinkle pink glitter onto wet paint as shown in Photo D. Let dry. Shake off extra glitter.

5 If the adhesive soaked through and the back side of your scarf is sticky, apply foil to those areas.

girls rock tie (page 65)

WHAT YOU NEED

Solid-color clip-on tie; foil adhesive
Crafting foil; fabric dimensional tube glitter paints
Glitter

HERE'S HOW

1 Use foil adhesive to draw the Girls Rock design (see photo on page 65) or other words. The adhesive will look milky white. When it is dry and ready for foiling it will appear clear and feel tacky. Be careful as you draw. You cannot wipe it off easily and the foil will stick wherever you put adhesive. Do not move to the next step before it dries; it is important to do these in order.

IF I EVER GET TO RIDE ON A MOTORCYCLE, I'M GONNA WEAR A SCARF ON MY HEAD!

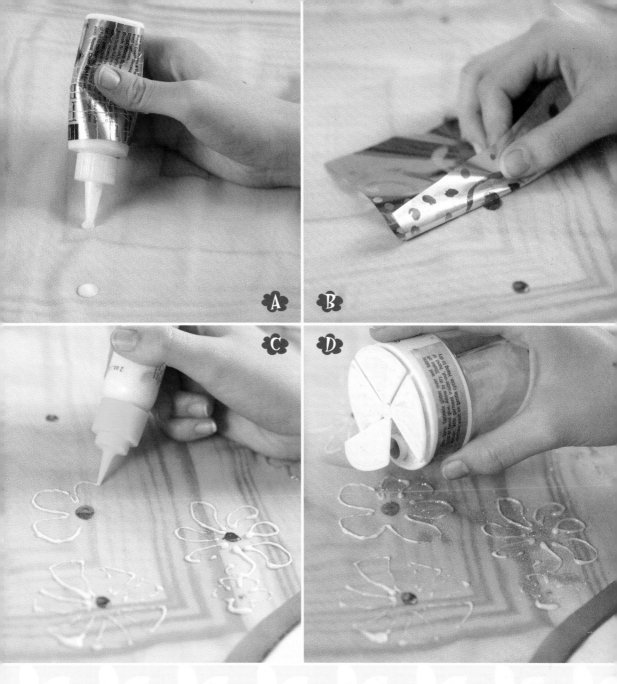

A

B

C

D

2 Lay dull side of foil onto tacky dry adhesive; rub it gently but firmly until all foil sticks to adhesive. Pull away the sheet, leaving the design foil-embossed.

3 If you want to use different colors of glitter on the tie design, use one color at a time. Draw with colored glitter paint and leave it that way or use fabric tube paint and sprinkle it with glitter. Let it dry and shake off excess glitter before drawing with more wet paint and adding a new color of glitter. Let dry. Shake off the extra glitter.

photo finish

Note: These shirts use two different kinds of transfer paper. To transfer to white fabric, you place the transfers image-side down and iron on the backing paper. To transfer to color fabric, you peel the backing off the transfer, place image-side up, cover with overlay paper, and then iron. Be sure to read the instructions that come with your transfer paper as the methods may be different.

personali-T (left)

WHAT YOU NEED

6¹/₂-inch square photograph

Iron-on photo transfer paper for white fabric, such as Hewlett-Packard iron-on transfers

Computer and color printer

continued on page 70

fashion. all over it!

Just think of all the neat things you can put on a shirt when you use iron-on transfers: your favorite quote; copies of your awards and badges—there's just no limit to what you can do!

HANGIN' OUT

Scanner or color copier; white cotton T-shirt
Scissors; iron; heart-shape pink gems
Permanent adhesive for gems, such as Gem-Tac

HERE'S HOW

1 Scan and print, or photocopy the photograph onto the transfer paper following the paper manufacturer's instructions. Keep in mind that the instructions may have you place the photo facedown on the shirt, which flops the image. If you want it to look like the original photo, choose "mirror image" when printing the copy.

2 Type your name on a computer, enlarging the letters to print about 2 inches high. Print your name onto the photo transfer paper, using the mirror-image setting if instructed by the paper manufacturer as shown in Photo A, opposite.

3 Using scissors, trim around the photo and the name.

4 Cover the ironing surface if instructed by the transfer paper manufacturer. Place the shirt on the surface. Center the trimmed photo and name papers on the shirt, making sure the letters will read correctly after the transfer.

5 Ask an adult to iron the back of the papers following the manufacturer's instructions as shown in Photo B. Let the paper cool. Peel off the paper backings.

6 Glue gems on the photo corners and to underline the name. Let dry.

it's-all-about-you shirt (page 69)

WHAT YOU NEED

Three photos, one at least 5$\frac{1}{2}$ inches square
Iron-on photo transfer paper, such as
   Hewlett-Packard iron-on transfers for color fabric
Yellow cotton sleeveless shirt; computer and printer
Scanner or color copier; circle cutter
Scissors; iron
Gems in a variety of shapes and colors
Permanent adhesive for gems, such as Gem-Tac

HERE'S HOW

1 Prepare the photographs following the instructions in Step 1, left. The paper used for the yellow shirt on page 69 did not require using the mirror-image setting.

2 Type your name in different colors on a computer four times using 1-inch type, and once vertically using 1$\frac{1}{4}$-inch type. Print your name on the photo transfer paper, again using the mirror- image setting if instructed by the paper manufacturer.

3 Ask an adult to help you use a circle cutter to trim around photos, as shown in Photo C or draw around a lid and cut out. Use scissors to cut out the printed names.

4 Cover the ironing surface if instructed by the transfer paper manufacturer. Place the shirt on the surface. Peel off the paper backing

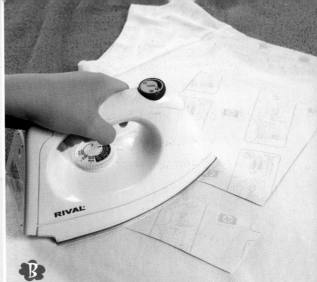

A B

C D

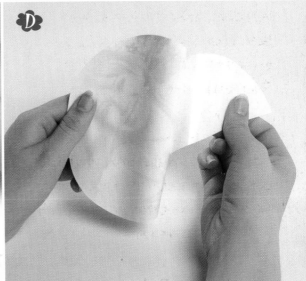

from the trimmed pieces as shown in Photo D.
Arrange the photos and names on the shirt.

5 Cover the transfers with the overlay paper.
Ask an adult to help you iron the transfers,
as shown in Photo E, following the manufacturer's
instructions. Let cool. Lift off the overlay paper.

6 Glue gems on and around the photos.
Let the glue dry.

E

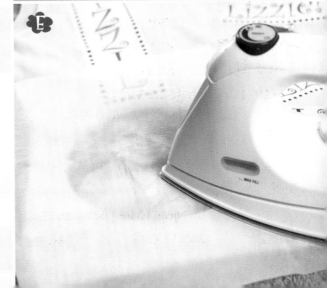

t-time

sweet cinch (left)

WHAT YOU NEED

Cotton scoop-neck shirt

Cardboard; small round lids

Pencil with eraser

Crafts sponges (available in crafts stores, these sponges are thin for cutting, then expand in water)

Scissors; paper plate; water

Glitter fabric paints in lime green and pink, or any colors you wish

White dimensional glitter fabric paint

continued on page 74

HANGIN' OUT

fashion. all over it!

T-shirts are so comfy to wear and so much fun to design! Once you've made your shirt, think about completing an outfit by decorating pants or a skirt to match!

HERE'S HOW

1 Wash and dry the shirt. Slip cardboard inside the shirt.

2 To make sponge stamps, trace around lids for circles, or draw petals, leaves, or other simple shapes. Cut out the shapes as shown in Photo B, opposite. Wet each sponge and squeeze out the excess water as shown in Photo C.

3 Place dabs of pink and green paint onto a plate. Thin with a little water if needed so they drip like cream. To practice stamping, dab a sponge into paint and then onto a scrap of paper. Make circle motifs around the neckline by alternating pink and green paints. Stamp a design in the center of the shirt. Let dry.

4 Dip the eraser end of a pencil in paint to make small circles. Outline the petals and large circles with white glitter paint. Let dry.

flower power t (page 73)

WHAT YOU NEED

T-shirt; cardboard; paper plate
Fabric paints in lime green, turquoise, yellow
   and magenta; water

Small sponge roller; pencil with eraser
Small round lids; flat expandable crafts sponge
Scissors; green glitter paint

HERE'S HOW

1 Wash and dry the T-shirt. Slip cardboard into the T-shirt.

2 Put about a teaspoon of green paint on a paper plate. Add about a teaspoon of water to it to make it thinner. Mix the paint and water.

3 Roll the small sponge roller in paint and then onto the front of the shirt to make stripes as shown in Photo A, opposite. Let dry.

4 To make sponge stamps, trace around lids for circles or draw petals, leaves, triangles, or other simple shapes. Cut out the shapes as shown in Photo B. Wet each sponge and squeeze out the excess water as shown in Photo C.

5 Place several quarter-size dabs of colored paint onto plate for painting flowers. Thin with a little water if needed so they drip like cream. To practice stamping, dab a sponge into paint and then onto a scrap of paper. Make simple flower shapes on the T-shirt by stamping dots, triangles, or teardrop shapes around a circle as shown in Photo D.

A B C D

6 Use the eraser end of a pencil to dip into paint and dot onto surface for smaller dots. Let dry.

7 For sparkle, outline areas with lime green glitter paint. Let dry.

fingernail fashion

WHAT YOU NEED

Fingernail polish

Straight pins

White paper

Toothpick

Small confetti and gems

HERE'S HOW

1 Start with clean, dry, unpolished fingernails. You can make the same design on every finger or make them different.

2 Paint each nail with polish. Let the polish dry.

continued on page 78

SCHOOL'S COOL

fashion, all over it!

Fingernail polish comes in a lot of colors—even metallics and some with glitter in them! Pick out some pretty hues and paint your finger- and toenails with awesome, artistic flair!

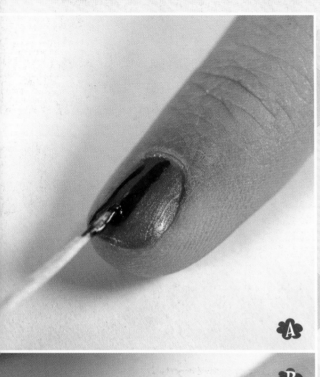

A

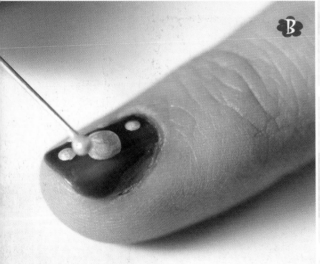
B

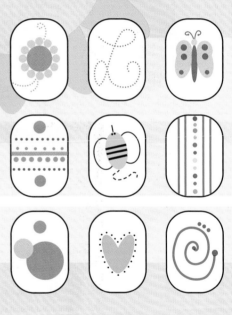

3 Use a piece of paper to experiment with the designs on pages 76-77 and below, or make up your own designs. Use a toothpick to draw stripes as shown in Photo A, left. To make dots, use the head of a straight pin as shown in Photo B.

4 While the polish is wet, press in confetti or gems if desired. Let the polish dry.

Buh-bye!

how to sew on a button

Cut off a length of thread. Guide the thread through the opening (eye) in the needle. Knot the ends of the thread.

Photo A: Insert the needle from the back of the fabric.

Photo B: Pull the needle to the front of the fabric.

Photo C: Pull thread until the knot is snug to the fabric back.

Photo D: Insert needle through one opening in the button.

Photo E: Slide button close to fabric. Insert needle in the other button hole and pull thread to the back.

Photo F: Repeat Steps D and E two or three times until the button is secure.

Photo G: Put the needle through the stitches on the back of the fabric at least three times to secure. Cut off the extra thread.

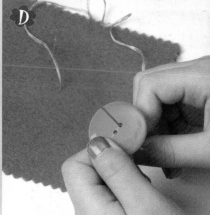

INDEX

I'M GOING TO HAVE THE COOLEST, MOST UNIQUE WARDROBE AROUND!